The woods hold not such another gem
as the nest of the hummingbird.
The finding of one is an event.

—John Burroughs, *naturalist*

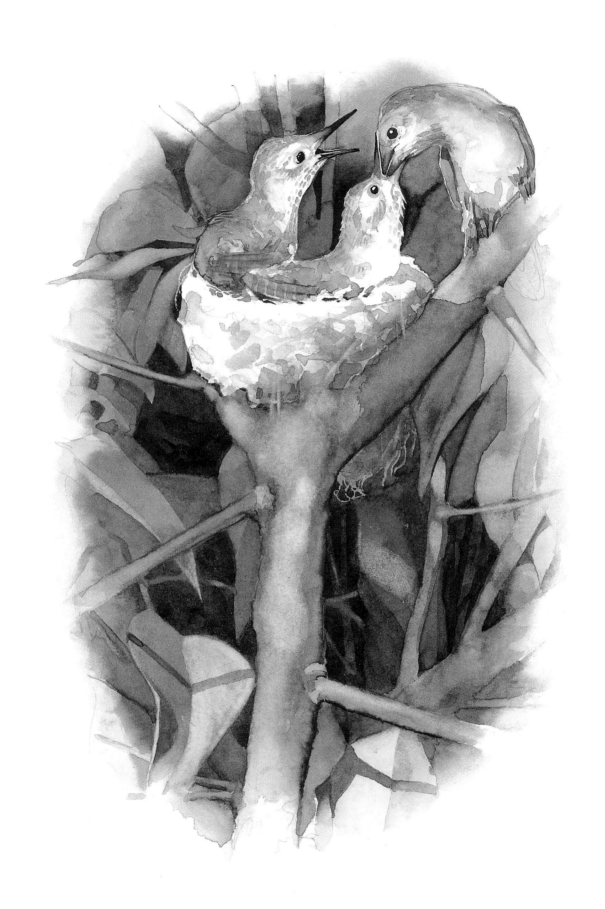

Hummingbird Nest

A JOURNAL OF POEMS

Kristine O'Connell George

ILLUSTRATED BY *Barry Moser*

HARCOURT, INC.

Orlando   Austin   New York   San Diego   Toronto   London

Many thanks to Ed Lewins, Curator of Birds at the San Diego Zoo, and to Shawnee Riplog Peterson,
Curator of Mammalogy and Ornithology at the Arizona-Sonora Desert Museum,
for reading this manuscript and generously sharing their expertise.
Thanks also to Kimball Garrett, Ornithology Collections Manager at the Natural History Museum
of Los Angeles County, Sheri L. Williamson of the Southeastern Arizona Bird Observatory,
and the hummingbird team at Project Wildlife for patiently answering my questions
about the growth and development of hummingbirds.
And, as always, my warmest thanks to Lynne T. Whaley for humming along with me.
—K. O. G.

Library of Congress Cataloging-in-Publication Data
George, Kristine O'Connell.
Hummingbird nest/Kristine O'Connell George; illustrations by Barry Moser.
p. cm.
Summary: When a mother hummingbird builds a nest on a family's porch, they watch and record her
actions and the birth and development of her fledglings.
1. Hummingbirds—Juvenile fiction. [1. Hummingbirds—Fiction.   2. Stories in rhyme.]
I. Moser, Barry, ill.   II. Title.
PZ8.3.G2937Hu 2004
[E]—dc21   99-50909
ISBN 0-15-202325-9

First edition
A C E G H F D B

Printed in Singapore

The illustrations in this book were done in transparent watercolor on paper.
The display lettering was created by John Stevens.
The text type was set in Zapf Renaissance Book.
Color separations by Colourscan Co. Pte. Ltd., Singapore
Printed and bound by Tien Wah Press, Singapore
This book was printed on 104gsm Cougar Opaque Natural paper.
Production supervision by Sandra Grebenar and Ginger Boyer
Designed by Barry Moser and Judythe Sieck

For my mother, with love
—K. O. G.

And for my grandson, Jacob Nathaniel James Martin
—*B. M.*

February 3

✿ VISITOR

A spark, a glint,
   a glimpse
   of pixie tidbit.
Bright flits, brisk zips,
   a green-gray blur,
   wings, zings, and *whirr*—

I just heard
   a humming of bird.

◈ Breakfast on the Patio

I see it from the corner of my eye,
   a feathered missile streaking by,
   aiming straight at me—

I duck, thinking an attack has begun.
   But wait, this *isn't* a squadron,
   it's only *one*

very small bird,

who abruptly hits invisible brakes,
   hovers midair in front of my face
   and orders:
               Get lost!
               Go away!
               I'm moving in today!

February 5

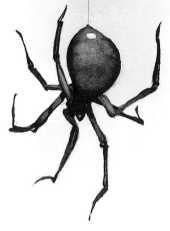

ℬ Spiders, Beware!

Mother is building
  her nest today.
Construction is already
  underway.

Spiders, beware!

Hummingbird's site
  was thoughtfully chosen
for a ready supply of webs,
  freshly woven.

✿ NEST CONSTRUCTION

Even after days of work,
she's still fussing, tucking—
feathers, cobwebs, a tuft
of silky grass.

Stepping lightly
around the edge,
she finally tries
it on for size,

checking to see
if it will fit
her sit.

February 7

✌ EXPECTANT

Our porch light shines
on an empty nest.
No one's home
tonight.
            I peek.

No eggs yet.

February 9

THE DOG COMPLAINS

That bird
is making a *mess*—
         splashing,
         flapping.
Water's flying—
         everywhere.
What *can* that bird be thinking?
         Bathtub?
         Swimming hole?
Out, bird!

         That's *my* bowl!

February 10

February 12

ℬ The Cat Remarks

I'm locked in jail,
can't go outside.
(I certainly tried.)
I'm a prisoner—
because of a bird.

How absurd.

✌ NEST CHECK

Can't resist, have to check
just once more today—
while the mother is away.

Cross my fingers,
hold my breath, hope,
peek into the nest,
whisper, *"Oh!"*

Something is beginning.
Two promises made—
two eggs newly laid.

February 22

♫ RAINY EVENING

Tonight, sitting on your nest,
almost unseen,
you are even slighter
than you seem
when you are
wide with flight.

You are silent
and serene
this rainy evening,
your quiet wings
smoothly pressed,
as you patiently sit,
gentle captain
     of your cobweb ship.

✏ JUST HATCHED

Each new
breath a shudder
as he huddles down deep
in the nest, head tucked in,
his body softly rounded,
warmly molded to the form
he once knew so well,
the smooth curved
world of shell.

February 27

CRACK!

Firstborn,
lying within those
woven walls of home,
under a feathered roof,
next to that warm smooth stone.

Did you think you were all alone?

Today,
that stone
cracked in two.
Suddenly, there was another,
perhaps a sister, maybe a brother.

Who *is* this, lying next to you?

March 1

✣ Nestlings

You're raisin black
and wrinkled.
Instead of feathered wings,
you're almost all head.
Don't worry, you are fine;
you're right in style.

So settle in,
stay with us awhile—
at least until
you're bigger than a dime.
This growing up stuff
is going to take time.

You're newly hatched;
you're newly alive.
We'll need to be patient
until those wings arrive.

✑ Helpless

Little thimble birds,
helpless, flightless,
and blind.
Don't know
that home
is fashioned
from webs and grass
lashed to a slender branch,
a delicate cup—

four feet up.

⌘ FINDING EGGSHELLS

Tidy housekeeper tosses
ivory scraps from the nest—
    empty cradles
    no bigger than
    my fingertip.

March 10

🐦 A Bird's-Eye View

At last,
they're big enough
to rest their tiny chins
on the rim and blink at the green
beyond.

March 11

➶ WARNING

Guarding her nest,
she chirps fiercely:

*Do not dare
mess with me
unless you wish
a taste of Fury,
for I am both
Judge and Jury.
Do not call me
teeny or petite.
I will conquer.
       I will defeat.*

✤ FEED ME! FEED ME!

Mother hummer leaves,
two thin beaks point toward sky—
exclamation points.

Mom returns with spider snacks—
open beaks, capital *V*s.

ℬ Flight Practice

Four curled feet grip
the top of the nest.
Two tiny motors
rev up for wing test.

Two aviators
begin to lift off....
                    Uh-oh!
They quickly adjust
wing speed back to *slow*....

Two student pilots
not yet ready
              to
                    let
                          go.

❧ Sky's Invitation

Fly up. Climb my blue,
catch a cloud or two.
I have plenty of room
for explorers like you.

March 20

✍ SOLO

You hopped to the edge,
   stepped over and out
   to a wide-open space
   you knew nothing about.
There was no going back,
   no looking down,
   no thought of falling
   or distant ground.
Was it an echo,
   a memory,
   or something you knew?

You stepped out.
               You flew.

✿ FAREWELL

I knew you could,
I wondered
when you would,
and now—
you are gone for good.

How did you know
you'd be the first to go?
How did you know
it was time to try
your wings and claim
your corner of sky?

I only wish
I'd said good-bye.

March 20

ஜ Left Behind

What will you dream tonight,
now that you are the only one?

Will you dream beginning?
Will you dream good-bye?
Will you dream

wings and sky?

March 22

&. Takeoff?

Tousled and rumpled,
scruffy, half finished,
he perches, flutters,
stumbles, falls out—

remembering wings
too late—

crash-lands
on a thin twig.
Holds *on.*

(Are his eyes
tightly shut?)

An hour later,
a long-distance flight:
six inches higher.

Little hunch of bird,
perches on a branch,
waiting, hoping,
that Mom shows up
with lunch.

March '22

✐ EMPTY NEST

They're gone.
No sign of them.
The time finally came.
My hummingbird family moved
away.

Tonight
the dark seems filled
with cold and cat and owl.
Pocket-sized birds sleeping, alone,
out there.

This is how
it's supposed to be.
So why do I keep watching
this empty nest in this empty tree?

ℬ Congratulations!

Well, Mom, you did it—
      you built the nest, laid the eggs,
      made a home, all on your own.
Thanks to you, your hatchlings enjoyed
      a full-service cafeteria,
      skybox view with premium seating,
      twenty-four-hour security patrol,
      climate control with central heating.
You were their umbrella in the rain,
      their awning in the sun.

Your babies have fledged.
      Your work is finally done.
      For all these weeks you faithfully
      manned your nesting station.
It's time, Mom—
              take a vacation!

March '23

New Visitors

Hummingbirds—
 tasting all the flowers
 draining the feeder
 hovering by the window
 zzit—zzit—zzit.
 Make a note: *Buy more sugar.*

Hummingbirds—
 zipping about our yard
 dizzying us
 appearing and disappearing
 dazzling us
 magicking all day long.

It's going to be
 a hummer
  of a summer!

April

AUTHOR'S NOTE

Tiny hummingbird
drinking from one red flower—
shakes the entire bush.

ONE WARM FEBRUARY MORNING, my family and I decided to eat breakfast on the patio of our home in Claremont, California. As soon as we sat down, a hummingbird flew repeatedly—at top speed—to within a few inches of our faces. Chirping furiously, the tiny bird dive-bombed us again and again. We finished breakfast inside!

We soon discovered the reason for the bird's aggressive behavior: She was building a nest in the ficus tree on our patio. That patio was *her* territory, and she was doing her best to defend her nesting area. Throughout the day, the bird would appear suddenly with a white tuft on the end of her beak, disappear briefly inside the leaves, and take off again. By late afternoon, a knot of nesting material the size of my thumb was attached to a branch.

For the next eight weeks I kept a "hummingbird journal," which evolved into this poetry collection. I still marvel over the surprising range of emotions one small bird and her family evoked: awe, worry about possible dangers, and laughter when the baby birds teetered on the edge of the nest for their daily flight practice.

The mother hummingbird was an iridescent green that glowed brightly in certain kinds of light, and she had a reddish patch on her chest. We identified her as an Anna's hummingbird, so we called her Anna. We tried to make Anna feel welcome by leaving a gift of shredded cotton balls—which she promptly wove into her nest. We shooed cats out of the yard and kept our dog inside the house as much as possible. The grass grew long and shaggy because we feared the noisy mower would frighten Anna away.

After her two eggs hatched, we would peek at the babies only when we knew that Anna was far from the nest. My daughter, Courtney, then eight years old, loved to watch from a stepladder we positioned about eight feet away. The ladder and a pair of binoculars made it possible for her to watch without disturbing the birds. Even though we knew precisely where the nest was located, we often had trouble spotting it because it was small— less than two inches in diameter—and elegantly camouflaged.

Although my reading had given me a rough idea of when the nestlings would be ready to leave the nest, I was still startled the day I discovered that one of the birds had gone. Determined not to miss seeing the second bird's first flight, I parked myself on the patio. By late afternoon of the second day, the tiny bird revved up its wings and let go of the edge of the nest. The brief solo from nest to branch was a bit bumpy, but one I'll always remember. The bird made two more short flights farther up into the tree before Anna returned with lunch. Shortly thereafter, they both disappeared from our yard.

What an empty feeling when our hummingbird drama was over! The events we'd seen on this diminutive stage had fascinated my family and our friends for many weeks. Anna was even responsible for many long-distance phone calls because my mother in Colorado requested daily hummingbird updates.

Looking at the empty nest, I knew we'd miss watching Anna and her babies' antics. After seeing our hummingbirds mature, it was easy for us to identify fledglings. Were any of the fledglings that turned up at our feeder later that spring *our* hummingbirds? I like to think they were.

—K. O. G.

More about Hummingbirds

ꕔ There are approximately 330 species of hummingbirds, all of which are native to the Western Hemisphere. Hummingbirds are the smallest birds in the world; they build the smallest nests and lay the smallest eggs. An Anna's hummingbird is 3½ to 4 inches long, and the eggs are approximately half an inch long.

ꕔ Naturalist John James Audubon described hummingbirds as "glittering fragments of the rainbow." If the light is just right, a hummingbird's iridescent feathers glitter and glow like jewels.

ꕔ The unique construction and "figure eight" movement of its wings allows a hummingbird to hover in midair like a helicopter. Hummers can also fly backward, sideways, and upside down, and do somersaults in midair. They rarely walk or hop because their feet are weak. If a hummingbird needs to get somewhere, it flies.

ꕔ In flight a hummingbird's wings look blurred because they beat so quickly—up to 200 beats a second. In the span of only a minute, a hummingbird takes approximately 250 breaths and its heart beats from 500 to 1,200 times. This amazingly fast metabolism requires hummingbirds to eat frequently, consuming up to half their weight in food each day.

ꕔ A hummingbird's beak may look like a straw, but the bird does not suck the nectar from flowers. Instead, its long tongue licks and absorbs the nectar. Spiders and insects are also an important part of a hummingbird's diet, supplying protein, fats, vitamins, and minerals.

ꕔ Hummingbirds are very territorial and protective of their nests and feeding areas. Hummers have been known to drive off much larger birds, including hawks.

Male hummingbirds are usually more brightly colored than females and are not involved in building nests or raising young. Their dramatic dive displays (up to 65 miles per hour from 60 to 120 feet in the air) are used to intimidate intruders and serve as courtship behavior prior to mating.

 Hummingbirds often choose sheltered locations for their nests; it is not unusual for an Anna's hummingbird to build her nest close to a house or under an eave. The female hummingbird uses plant materials and spiderwebs, which she camouflages to blend in with the surroundings. As the hatchlings mature, the supple nest stretches to fit the growing birds.

 The female hummingbird usually lays two eggs, a day or so apart, and incubates them for 15 to 17 days. Most eggs hatch in 14 to 23 days.

 Born blind and without feathers, hummingbird hatchlings slowly open their eyes and begin to grow feathers in their first few weeks. Anna's hatchlings stay in the nest, where the mother feeds, protects, and warms them, for 18 to 26 days. The mother even shades her babies with her wings on hot days.

 The mother hummingbird feeds her hatchlings a mixture of nectar, small insects, and spiders several times an hour. She partially digests the food in her crop, inserts her beak into the hatchling's mouth, and regurgitates the meal.

 Once they are strong enough, the baby hummingbirds practice for the day they will fly by perching on the edge of the nest and exercising their wings.

 Young hummingbirds that have left the nest are called fledglings. The mother stays close to her nearly independent fledglings and continues to care for them until they grow stronger and can feed themselves. New fledglings are a dull color. However, by the following nesting season, most young hummers have acquired their brightly colored iridescent feathers.

Books about Hummingbirds

For young readers:

Dancers in the Garden by Joanne Ryder, with illustrations by Judith Lopez.
San Francisco, Calif.: Sierra Club Books for Children, 1992.

Hummingbirds: A Beginner's Guide by Laurel Aziz. Toronto, Ontario, Can.:
Firefly Books, 2002.

Hummingbirds: Jewels in the Sky by Esther Quesada Tyrrell, with photographs
by Robert A. Tyrrell. New York: Crown Publishers, 1992.

The Hungry Hummingbird by April Pulley Sayre, with illustrations by Gay W. Holland.
Brookfield, Conn.: Millbrook Press, 2001.

It's a Hummingbird's Life by Irene Kelly. New York: Holiday House, 2003.

For older readers:

A Field Guide to Hummingbirds of North America (Peterson Field Guides)
by Sheri L. Williamson. Boston, Mass.: Houghton Mifflin Company, 2002.

A Hummingbird in My House: The Story of Squeak by Arnette Heidcamp.
New York: Crown Publishers, 1991.

Hummingbirds: Jewels in Flight by Connie Toops. Stillwater, Minn.: Voyageur Press, 1992.

The Hummingbirds of North America by Paul A. Johnsgard, with color plates
by Mark Marcuson, James McClelland, and Sophie Webb. Washington, D.C.:
Smithsonian Institution Press, 1997.

Hummingbirds, Their Life and Behavior: A Photographic Study of the North American Species by
Esther Quesada Tyrrell, with photographs by Robert A. Tyrrell. New York:
Crown Publishers, 1985.

The Secret Lives of Hummingbirds by David Wentworth Lazaroff, with photographs by Paul
and Shirley Berquist. Tucson, Ariz.: Arizona-Sonora Desert Museum Press, 1995.

Stokes Beginner's Guide to Hummingbirds by Donald and Lillian Stokes. New York:
Little, Brown and Company, 2002.

The World of the Hummingbird by Robert Burton. Toronto, Ontario, Can.: Firefly
Books, 2001.

The World of the Hummingbird by Harry Thurston. San Francisco, Calif.: Sierra
Club Books, 1999.